Origami
AIRCRAFT

JAYSON MERRILL

DOVER PUBLICATIONS, INC.
MINEOLA, NEW YORK

Introduction

Origami purists have few choices when making origami aircraft. With this book I hope to change that. The aircraft in this book are all made from squares and are all fully functional. They all fly, have landing gear that retract, cockpits that open, and cannons that swivel. However, all of this detail and functionality come at a price. The aircraft can all be hard to make, difficult to fly, and sometimes seemingly impossible to balance. This book was written with the experienced folder in mind, but anyone looking for a challenge is welcome. How to fly these planes will be explained later, but everyone will find their own way to fly them.

For these aircraft you must use very lightweight paper due to their compact design. Some aircraft require you to use tracing paper, while others require paper that is at least 15-weight, usually graph paper or notebook paper. You can find these papers nearly anywhere. When reading the diagrams you must pay close attention to the step you are on and the step afterward. This will help you get an idea of what's coming. If some of your aircraft are performing badly, they may need to be balanced. This will be explained later.

I have spent many hours with this book and the aircraft and I hope that you will spend as much time on them too. Good luck!

Bibliographical Note

Origami Aircraft is a new work, first published by
Dover Publications, Inc., in 2006.

International Standard Book Number

ISBN-13: 978-0-486-45062-9
ISBN-10: 0-486-45062-7

Manufactured in the United States by Courier Corporation
45062709   2014
www.doverpublications.com

Table of Contents

Symbols and Signs, 4

Basic Procedures, 5

Aircraft

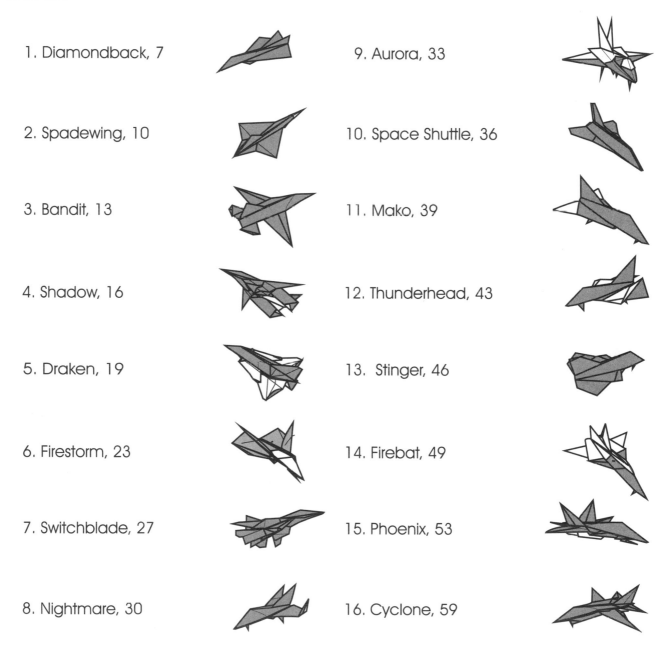

Flight Instructions, 61

Symbols and Signs

Lines

————————	An edge
————————	A highlighted crease or edge
————————	A crease
··················	A hidden edge or crease
··················	A hidden fold
- - - - - - - - - -	A valley fold
-·-·-·-·-·-·-·-	A mountain fold

Arrows

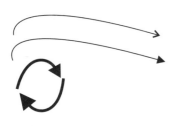

The direction of the fold

Three dimensional folding

Turn the model over

Grab or push

Fold and unfold

Fold over and over

Repeat a process on another part of the model

Basic Procedures

Squash-fold

 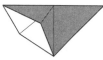

Open the two layers and bring the point down.

In progress.

Completed.

Rabbit-ear-fold

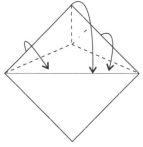 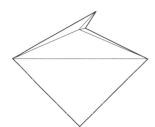 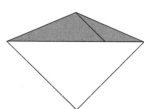

Bring the two sides to the center while pinching the top of the triangle.

In progress.

Completed.

Inside-reverse-fold

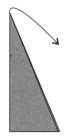 

Open the two sides out while pushing the point in.

Completed.

Swivel-fold

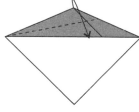 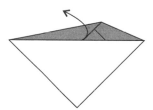 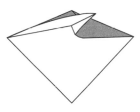

Take both layers of paper and unfold them to where the last fold was. The paper won't lie flat.

In progress.

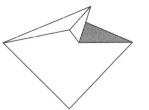

Completed.

Petal-fold

 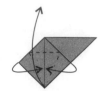

Fold then unfold the sides in.

Using the creases you just made, swing the bottom flap up and push the sides in.

In progress.

Completed.

Jet-fold

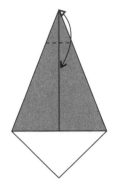 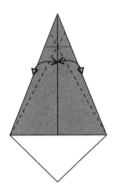 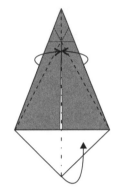 

Fold, then unfold.

Fold, then unfold using the crease you just made.

Push the sides in using the creases you just made while letting the bottom of the paper come out.

In progress. Note when you flatten the model, lie it flat on its side.

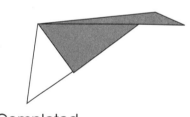

Completed.

Diamondback

Use a 7 - 9 in square of 15-weight paper.

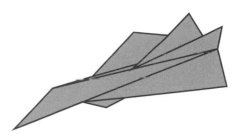

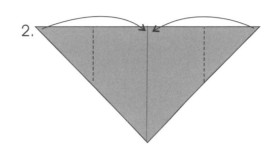

1.

2.

3.

4.

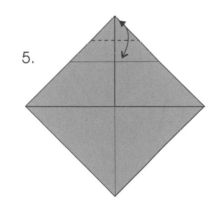

5.

6.

Fold then unfold.

Fold then unfold.

7.

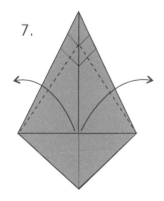

8.

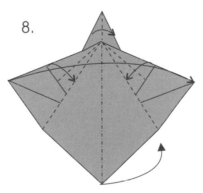

9.

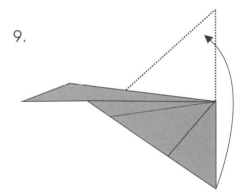

Fold the flaps out, taking
the paper underneath with
them.

Fold the small flaps in half.
Then, jet-fold the model.

Fold the inner
flap straight up.

10.

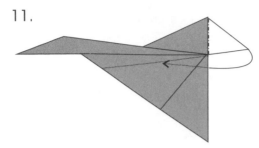

Fold the top of the tail fin into the hidden edge.

11.

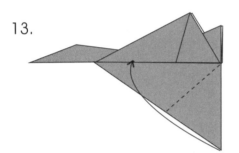

Fold the small triangle into the tail fin so that it makes two separate flaps.

12.

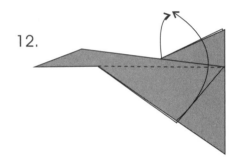

13.

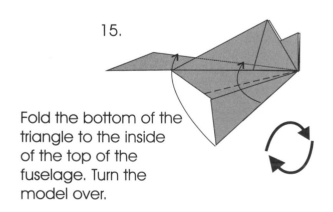

Fold the tip of the triangle to the point shown on the bottom of the keel.

14.

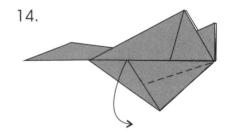

Fold the new triangle in half.

15.

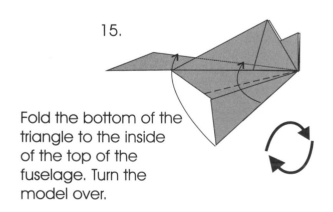

Fold the bottom of the triangle to the inside of the top of the fuselage. Turn the model over.

16.

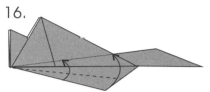

Fold the bottom of the triangle to the inside of the top of the fuselage to form the keel.

17.

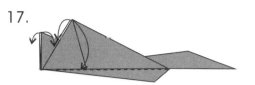

Fold the wings and tail fins to the angles shown in step 17A.

17A.

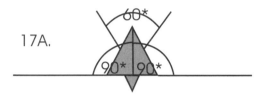

Note: Make sure that the forward edges of the wings are straight, otherwise the plane will pull to one side or the other.

18.

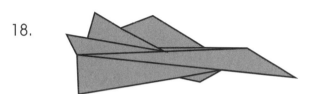

Hold the middle of the keel and give the plane a smooth, straight throw for maximum performance. The plane will fly smoothly, straight, and fast with a good range.

Spadewing

Use a 7 - 9 inch square of 15-weight paper.

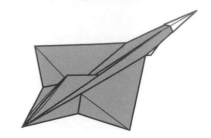

1.
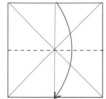

2.
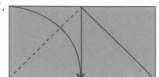

3.
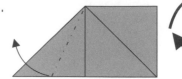

Squash-fold the flap. Then turn the model over.

4.
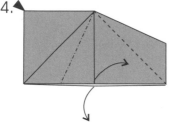

Squash-fold.

5.
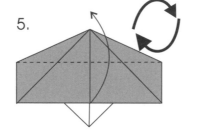

Fold the paper up then turn the model over.

6.
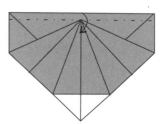

7.
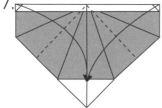

8.
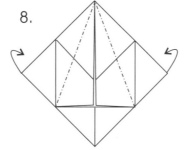

Fold the two sides behind and swing the excess paper out. Turn the model over.

9.
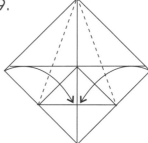

10.
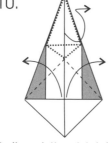

Pull out the hidden flap from the inside.

11.
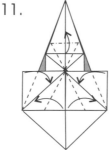

12.
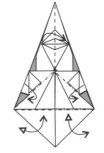

Valley-fold one of the bottom triangles to the front and one to the back, then unfold them. Fold the two side flaps underneath. Fold one flap from the top triangle over.

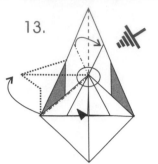

13.

Swivel the wing upward and inward, using the marked intersection.

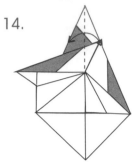

14.

Fold one flap over and unfold.

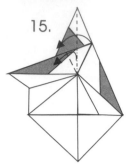

15.

Swivel the flap out and downward.

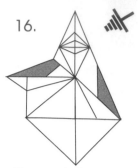

16.

Repeat steps 12 to 16 on the other side.

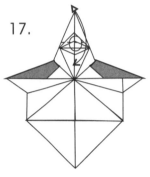

17.

Fold the nose down, and unfold through the point indicated.

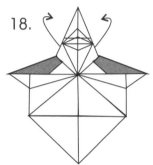

18.

Wrap the top flaps of the top triangle inside the pockets underneath.

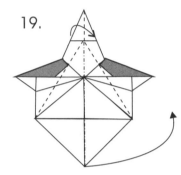

19.

Jet-fold the model as shown.

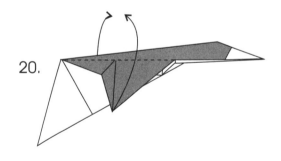

20.

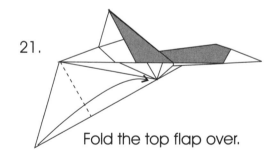

21.

Fold the top flap over.

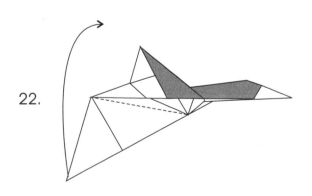

22.

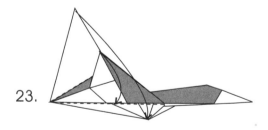

23.

Fold the remaining flap into the tail fin to lock the model. Fold the wings out as shown in step 24.

24.

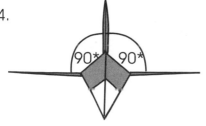

Fold the wings out 90* from the keel.

25.

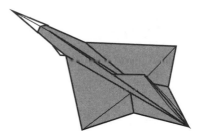

Hold the front of the keel and give the plane a smooth throw. Make sure the edges of the wings and the tail fins are straight.

Bandit

Use a 7 - 9 inch square of 15-weight paper.

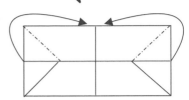

1.
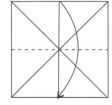

2.
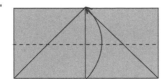

3.
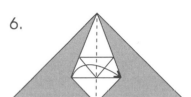

Inside-reverse-folds.

4.
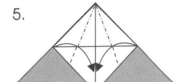

Inside-reverse-folds.

5.

Squash-folds.

6.

Fold one flap over.

7.
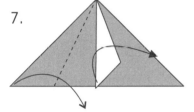

Swivel-fold the flap out;
then fold the side in.

8.
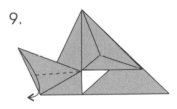

9.

10.
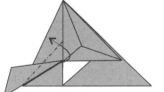

Fold the edge noted
underneath itself.

11.

12.
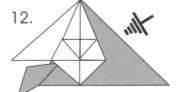

Repeat steps 6 - 12 on
the opposite side.

13.
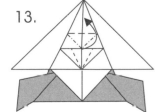

Petal-fold.

14.
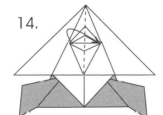

Fold one flap over.

15.
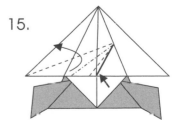

Squash-fold the flap while
folding the small excess noted
over the top of the fold.

13

16.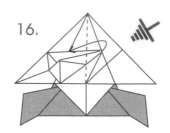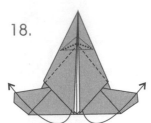

Fold one flap over, then repeat steps 14 - 16 on the other side.

17.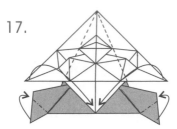

Fold the two tail fins into the pockets behind and along the inner edge. Then fold the wings down.

18.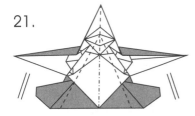

Fold the wings out using the preexisting crease underneath.

19.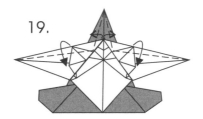

Swivel-fold the top edges of the wings down.

20.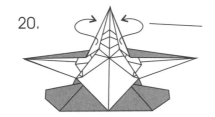

Wrap the two top side edges underneath the triangle below.

21.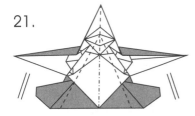

Fold the rear of the fuselage down and inward, parallel to the outside of the fuselage, using the crease used in step 18.

22.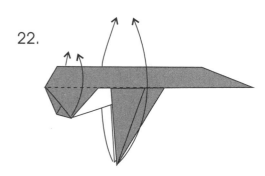

23.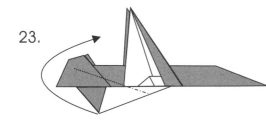

Inside-reverse-fold the middle flap up to form the tail.

24.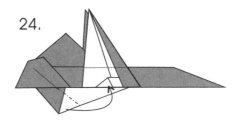

Fold the two flaps together into the top of the fuselage.

25.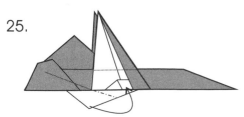

Fold the two flaps together into the top of the fuselage.

26.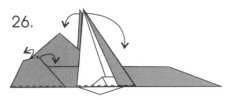

Open the fuselage as shown in step 28. Then fold the wings down as shown in step 27.

27.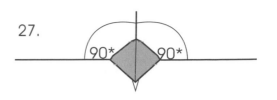

28.

Hold the middle of the keel and give the plane a smooth toss for maximum performance. The plane will fly smoothly with good maneuverability.

Shadow

Use a 7 - 10 inch square of 15-weight paper.

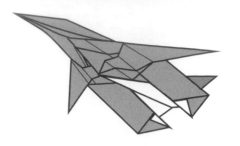

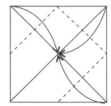
1.

2.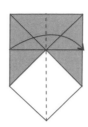

Fold in half, then
rotate 90*.

3.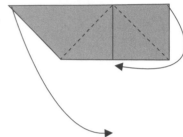

4.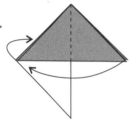

Fold the large
flap behind and
the small one to
the front.

5.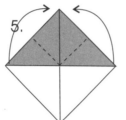

6.

Fold and unfold,
then turn the model
over.

7.

Petal-fold.

8.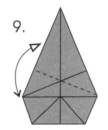

Fold and
unfold.

9.

Fold and
unfold.

10.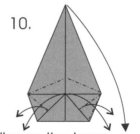

Collapse the large
triangle down and out,
using the existing creases.

11.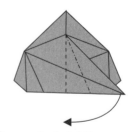

Squash-fold the
flap.

12.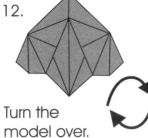

Turn the
model over.

13.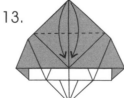

14.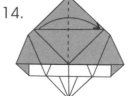

Fold one flap
over.

15.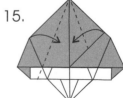

16

16.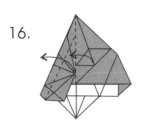

Fold the wing over so that the bottom edge folds directly over the corner that is adjacent to it. Then fold one flap over.

17.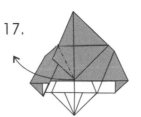

Fold the flap over along the existing creases.

18.

Repeat steps 14 - 17 on the other side.

19.

Inside-reverse-fold the inner triangle straight up.

20.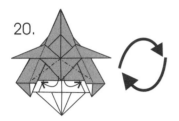

Using the inner edge of the fuselage as a guide, mountain-fold the two flaps inside. Then turn the model over.

21.

Mountain-fold the excess into the pocket behind. Then turn the model over.

22.

Fold the nose down to the intersection shown and unfold.

23.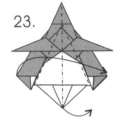

Jet-fold the model using the crease made and the intersections of the wings and the fuselage.

24.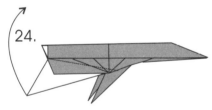

Using the intersection of the white and the colored part of the keel and the trailing edges of the wings, fold the tail fin up.

25.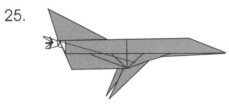

Fold the small excess flaps into the tail fin as far as they will go. Then open out the fuselage 90 degrees from the keel and pinch the nose.

26.

Fold the two flaps together to the top of the fuselage.

27.

Fold the two flaps together to the top of the fuselage. Again to lock the model into place.

28.

Pull out the paper behind and under the nose to form the air intakes as shown in step 29.

29.

Hold the front of the keel and give the plane a smooth toss. It will fly smoothly and will maneuver easily.

Draken

Use a 8 - 10 inch square of 15-weight paper.

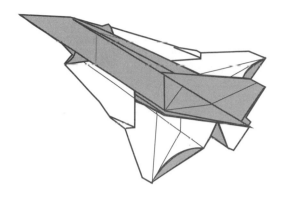

1.

2.
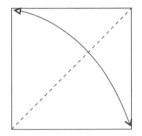

3.
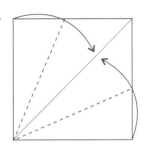

4.
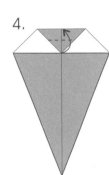

5.
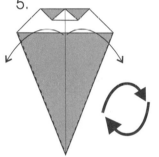

Fold the flaps down, then turn the model over.

6.
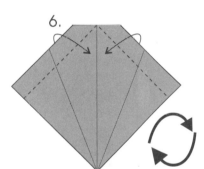

Fold the two sides in, then turn the model over.

7.
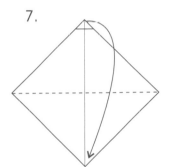

8.
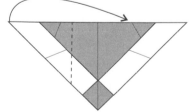

9.

Squash-fold, then unfold to step 8. Repeat steps 8 - 9 on the other side.

10.
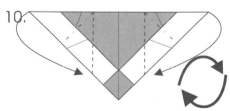

Squash-fold on the existing creases, then turn the model over.

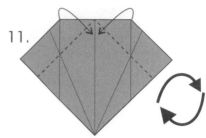

11.

Fold the top edges into
the middle of the model,
then turn it over.

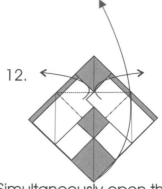

12.

Simultaneously open the two
sides out and swing the
bottom flap up.

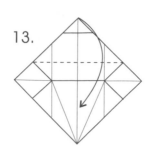

13.

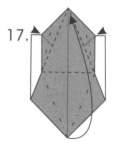

14.

Fold the flap into the
pocket behind it. Then
turn the model over.

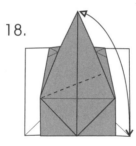

15.

Fold the two sides in,
then turn the model
over.

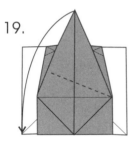

16.

Simultaneously fold the
sides in and swing the
paper behind out. Then
turn the model over.

17.

First squash-fold the two
flaps, then petal-fold
the bottom flap up.

18.

Fold, then unfold

19.

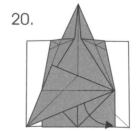

20.

Pull the paper from
underneath out.

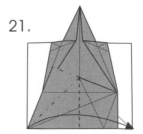

21.

Rabbit-ear fold the
flap over.

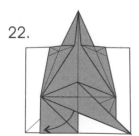

22.

Pull the paper from
underneath out.

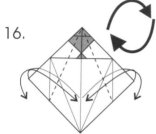
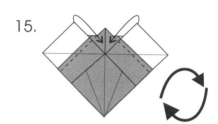

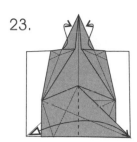

23.

Fold and unfold the bottom flap. Then place the excess of the squash-fold behind the top layer of paper.

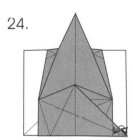

24.

Fold, then unfold the tip of the bottom flap to the edge behind it. Then turn the model over.

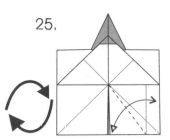

25.

Fold the flap over from the center of the model and from the edge behind it.

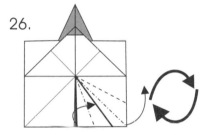

26.

Swivel the bottom flap until the line from the inside edge lies over the diagonal line on the edge behind it. Then turn the model over. See step 29

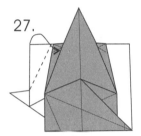

27.

Fold the side over and tuck the corner under the top layers.

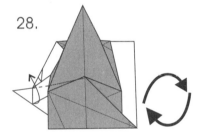

28.

Fold the flap made in step 24 up all the way from the inside of the model. Then turn the model over.

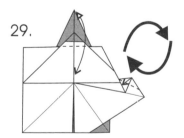

29.

Fold the top down, then unfold. Fold the small section of the wing down. Then turn the model over.

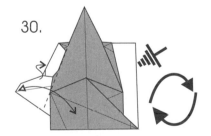

30.

Tuck the layer you just folded inside the small pocket behind it. Then fold and unfold the wing. Repeat steps 24 - 28 on the other side and turn the model over

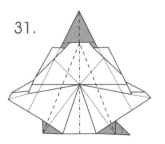

31.

Jet-fold the model as shown.

32.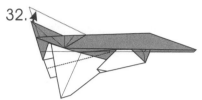

Pull the tail up until it lines up with the intersections shown in step 31. The very middle of the tail fin will form a box pleat.

33.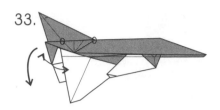

Notice where the small circles are. This is how the intersections should look. Inside-reverse-fold the tip of the tail fin on the existing crease. Then open the back of the model out so that the underside is facing you.

34.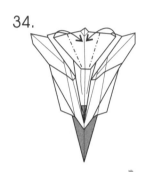

Fold the innermost flaps in to the tail fin, then slightly close the model.

35.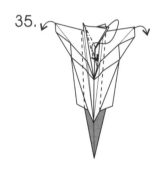

Fold the two flaps over and over together into the interior of the model. Then fold the wings parallel to the fuselage. Rotate the plane so that the back is facing you.

36.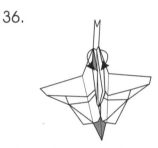

Round the two flaps to form an afterburner. Then rotate the model so the front is facing you.

37.

Round the edges shown to form air intakes.

38.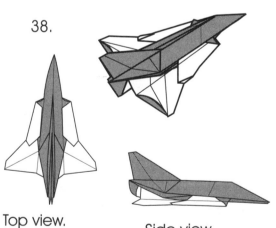

Top view.

Side view

Firestorm

Use a 7 - 9 inch square of 15-weight paper.

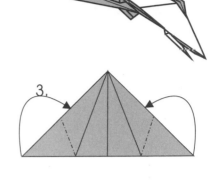

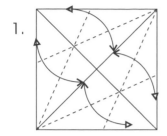 1.

Fold then
unfold.

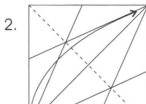 2.

Fold in half, then
rotate 45*.

3.

Inside-reverse-fold the
two edges in.

4.

Fold then unfold.
Repeat behind.

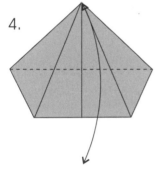 5

Make a preliminary fold
using the creases you
just made. Repeat
behind.

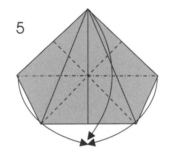 6.

7.

Fold one flap over.

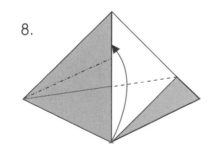 8.

Squash fold.

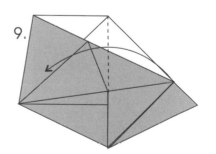 9.

Fold one flap over.

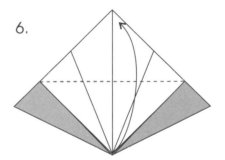

23

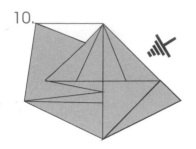

10.

Repeat steps 7 - 10 on the opposite side.

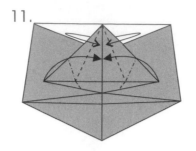

11.

Swivel fold the two edges of the flap on top of the flap.

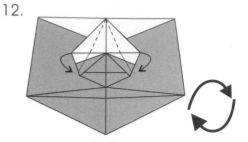

12.

Fold the two sides of the flap into the middle and behind the flap. Then turn the model over.

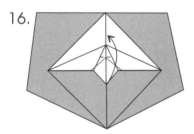

13.

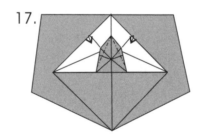

14.

Rabbit-ear-fold.

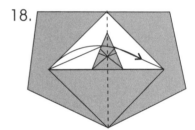

15.

Squash-fold.

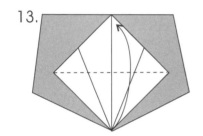

16.

Pull the flap up as far as it will go and flatten it.

17.

Fold the sides underneath.

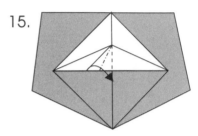

18.

Fold one flap over.

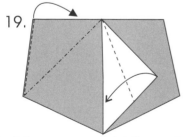

19.

Inside-reverse-fold the outer edge. Then valley-fold the flap in half.

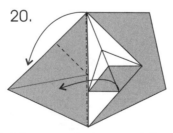

20.

Fold the newly formed flap down as far as it will go straight along the outer edge. Then fold the flap back over.

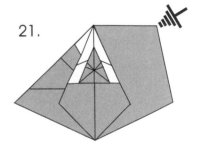

21.

Repeat steps 18 - 21 on the opposite side.

22.

Turn the model over.

23.

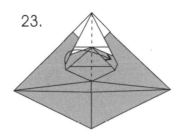

Fold one flap over.

24.

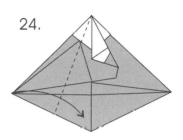

25.

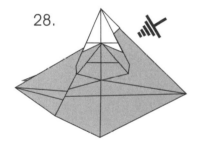

Let this flap swing
out, then flatten it.

26.

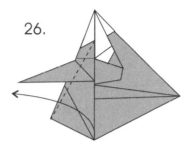

27.

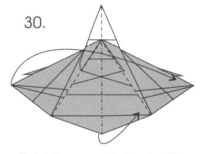

Fold one flap over.

28.

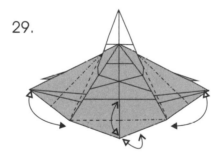

Repeat steps 23 - 28
on the opposite side.

29.

Squash-fold the wings and then
unfold them. Fold one of the
small flaps straight to the front
and one to the back, then
unfold them.

30.

Fold the model in half
while folding the
middle inward using
the inside edges of the
wings as a guide. Then
rotate 90°.

31.

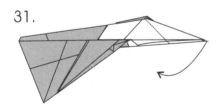

Inside-reverse-fold the
inner flap.

32.

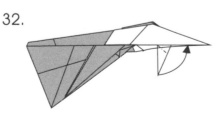

Inside-reverse-fold the flap
back up.

33.

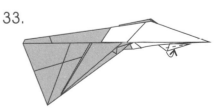

Narrow the flap by valley
folding the sides up.

34.

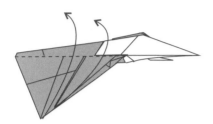

Fold the canard wings and the wings up.

35.

Fold the two flaps over together.

36.

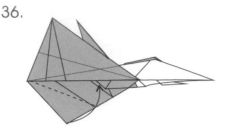

Fold the flap to the top of the inside of the fuselage.

37.

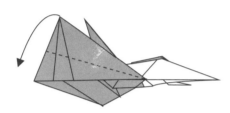

Squash fold the wings down, and fold the canard wings down with them as shown in step 38.

38.

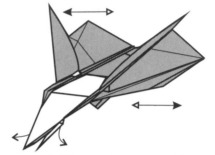

This aircraft has additional features. The wings can fold closer to or farther from the fuselage, affecting the way the plane flies. The farther the wings are from the keel, the more maneuverable the plane will be; the closer they are, the faster it will fly. The small cannon underneath the nose can also move. For best performance, hold the craft on the front of the keel to throw it.

Switchblade

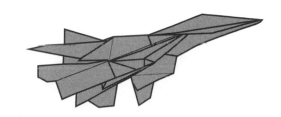

Use a 8 - 10 inch square of tracing paper.

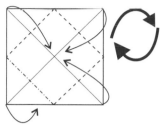

1.

Fold three corners to the front and one to the back. Then turn the model over.

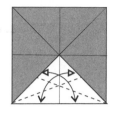

2.

Fold, then unfold.

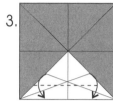

3.

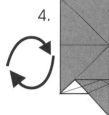

4.

Turn the model over.

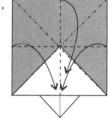

5.

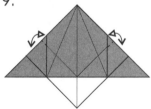

6.

Fold, then unfold.

7.

Fold, then unfold.

8.

9.

Fold, then unfold.

10.

11.

12.

Fold one flap to the front and one to the back.

13.

14.

15.

16.

Repeat steps 13 - 16 on the other side.

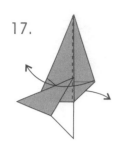

17.

Fold one flap to the front and one to the back.

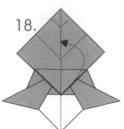

18.

Inside-reverse-fold the inner paper.

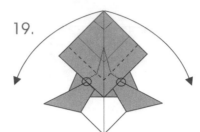

19.

Swivel-fold the two flaps straight down so that the bottom edge lies on the intersection noted.

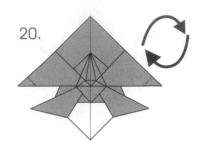

20.

Turn over.

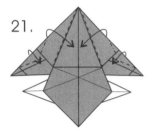

21.

Swivel-fold the wings as shown.

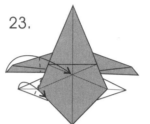

22.

Put the layers of paper made in step 21 inside the model.

23.

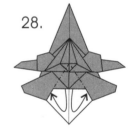

24.

Fold the tip of the tail fin to the hidden edge underneath. Then fold the wing straight over as shown.

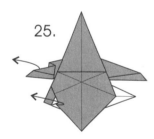

25.

Unfold to step 23.

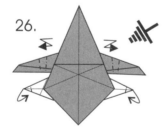

26.

Using the creases made in steps 23 - 25, inside-reverse-fold the wing and the tail fin. Repeat this on the opposite side.

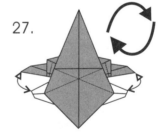

27.

Swivel-fold the wingtips down to the tail fins, then swivel them back. Turn the model over.

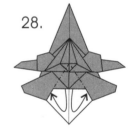

28.

Fold the small flaps underneath.

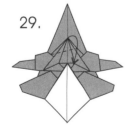

29.

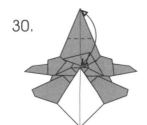

30.

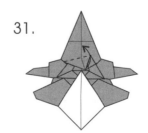

31.

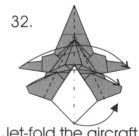

32.

Jet-fold the aircraft, then rotate 90°.

33.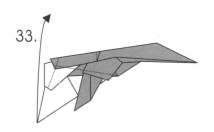

Inside-reverse-fold the tail fin straight up from the inside of the edge inside the keel.

34.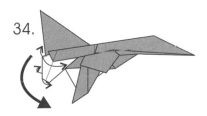

Partially open the back of the model to expose the inside of the tail fin and rotate the model so the rear of the aircraft is facing you.

35.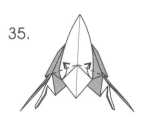

Fold the excess of the tail fin up. Then rotate the model so that the underside is facing you.

36.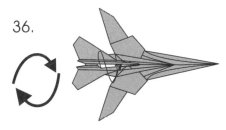

Fold the flap into the fuselage to lock the model. Then turn the model over.

37.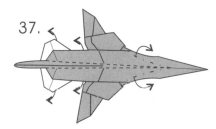

Open the fuselage out along the wings so that the wings are perpendicular to the keel. At the same time pinch the nose and round the part of the fuselage as noted.

38.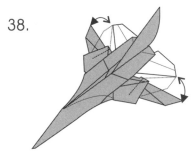

This is what the model should look like. You can swivel the wings back and forth for extra maneuverability.

Front view.

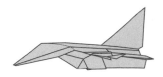

Side view.

Nightmare

Use a 8-11 inch square of 15-weight paper.

1.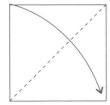

2.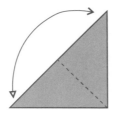

Fold, then unfold.

3.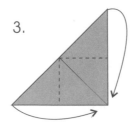

4.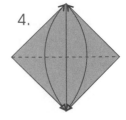

Fold, then unfold.

5.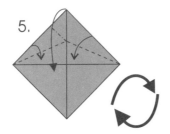

Rabbit-ear-fold, then turn the model over.

6.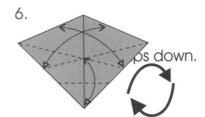

ps down.

Fold, then unfold. Then turn the model over.

7.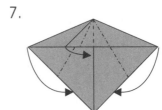

Squash-fold the sides in underneath the two top points. Then squash-fold the small top triangle.

8.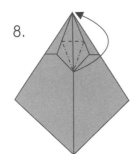

Petal-fold.

9.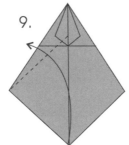

10.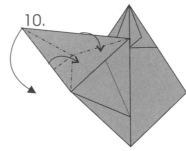

Rabbit-ear-fold.

11.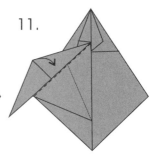

12.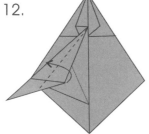

13.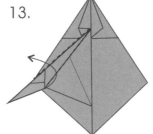

14.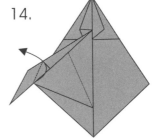

Open out the wing and squash-fold the pocket that forms.

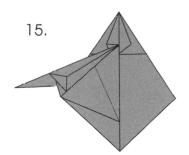

15.

Unfold the wing to
step 10.

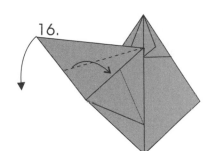

16.

Squash-fold.

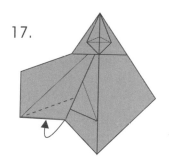

17.

Inside-reverse-fold
this side only.

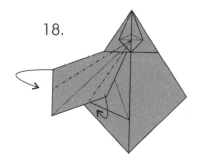

18.

Mountain-fold the sides
inward.

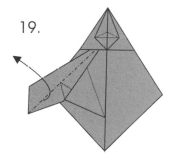

19.

Using the folds made in
step 15, push the middle
crease out and squash-fold
the inner pocket.

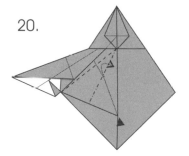

20.

Squash-fold the flap
and keep the inner
layer of paper to the
inside of the model.

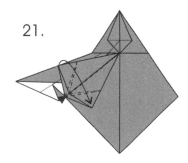

21.

Petal-fold the flap, then
fold it in half.

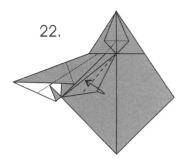

22.

Fold the edge over.

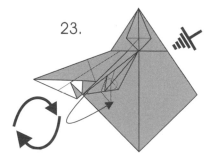

23.

Inside-reverse-fold the
small flap straight down
using the inner edge and
the intersection noted.
Repeat steps 9 - 23 on tho
opposite side, then turn
the model over.

24.

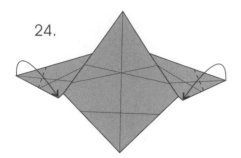

Fold the wing tips in, then turn the model over.

25.

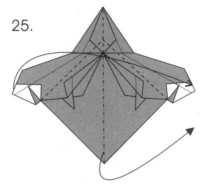

Jet-fold the aircraft using the intersections shown.

26.

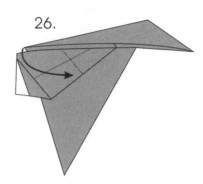

Open out the back of the model so the creases made earlier can be seen.

27.

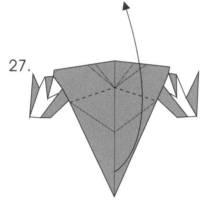

Using preexisting creases as a guide, inside-reverse-fold up.

28.

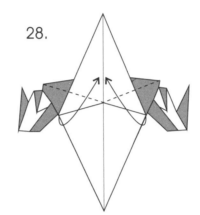

Fold the sides of the flap in. Then close the model and return it to the same position as in step 26.

29.

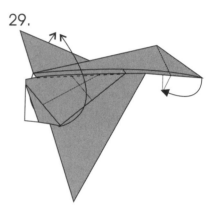

Fold the wings straight up. Inside-reverse-fold the flap under the nose down.

30.

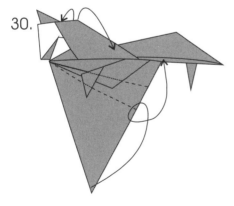

Fold the bottom flap into the model to lock it. Then fold the wing down and the wingtips out as shown in step 31.

31.

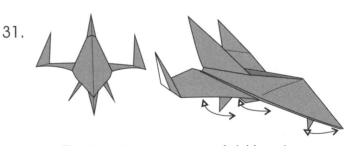

The landing gear can fold back into the aircraft for flight and can be redeployed for landing. To fly the plane, hold the back of the keel by the landing gear and give it a hard, smooth throw.

Aurora

Use an 8-10 inch square of 15-weight paper.

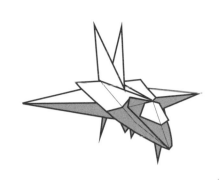

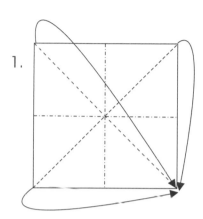

1.

Form a preliminary fold.

2.

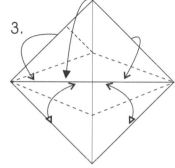

3.

Rabbit-ear-fold the top flap, then fold and unfold the bottom flaps.

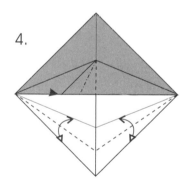

4.

Squash-fold the small flap then fold and unfold the bottom flaps as shown.

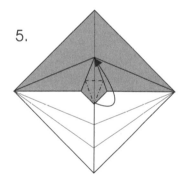

5.

Petal-fold the flap up.

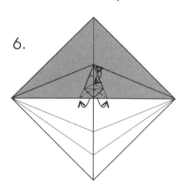

6.

Fold and unfold the top flap. Fold the excess paper under as shown.

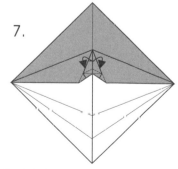

7.

Outside-reverse-fold the flap using the crease you just made.

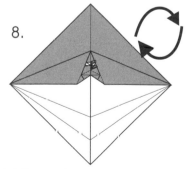

8.

Fold the edge down and swing the paper behind it out. Then turn the model over.

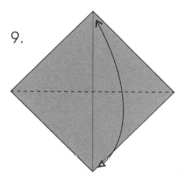

9.

Fold, then unfold.

10.

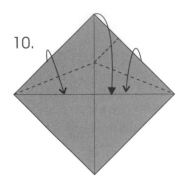

Rabbit ear-fold the top triangle.

11.

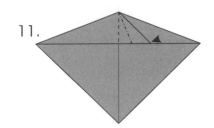

Squash-fold the flap.

12.

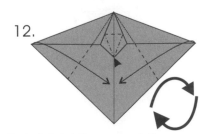

Petal-fold the small flap. Fold only the inside layers to the middle, then turn the model over.

13.

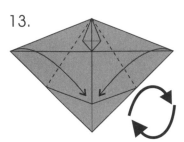

Fold the sides in, then turn the model over.

14.

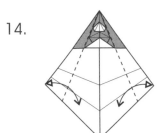

Fold, then unfold.

15.

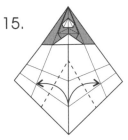

Fold the flaps back on themselves on the lines, using the intersections shown.

16.

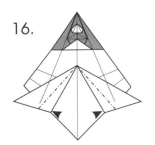

Using the line behind the flaps, inside-reverse-fold the excess paper. Then turn the model over.

17.

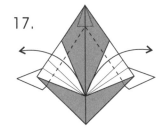

Using the inside flap and the line made in step 12 as a guide, fold the wings out.

18.

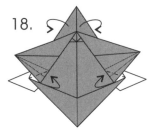

Fold the corner of the wings under, then place the wings under the flaps behind them.

19.

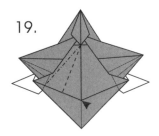

Squash-fold this flap.

20.

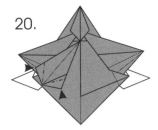

Inside-reverse-fold the sides.

21.

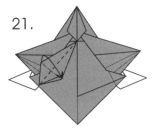

22.

Inside-reverse-fold the flap straight down. Then repeat steps 18 - 21 on the other flap.

23.

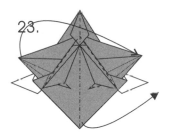

Jet-fold the model.

24.

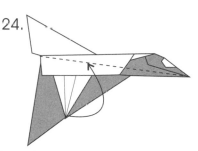

Fold the wings up perpendicular to the fuselage.

25.

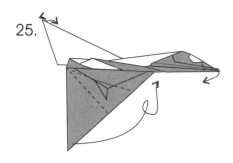

First inside-reverse-fold the small flap under the nose down from just below the cockpit. Then fold the bottom flap into the model to lock it. Slightly spread the tail fins apart.

26.

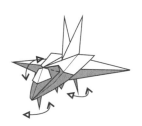

The landing gear can fold up and down. The cockpit can open and close. To fly this plane, hold the keel at the back by the landing gear and give it a hard throw. This plane can fly well in heavy winds.

Space Shuttle

Use an 8 - 11 inch square of tracing paper.

1.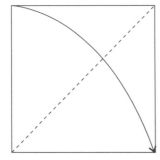

2.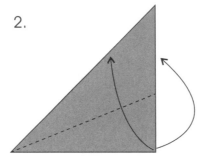

3.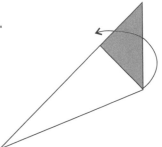

Open out the paper and turn it upright.

4.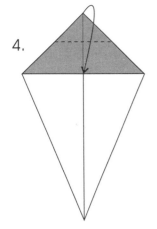

5.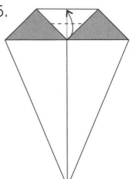

6.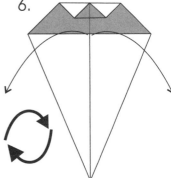

Fold the flaps down, then turn the model over.

7.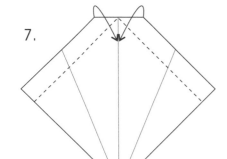

8.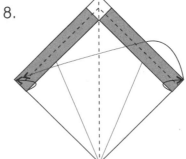

First valley-fold the sides in, then fold the paper in half.

9.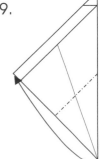

Inside-reverse-fold as shown.

10.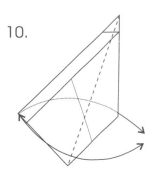

Fold the flap behind over. Fold and unfold the front flap.

11.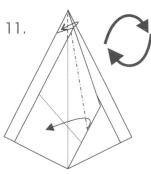

Simultaneously fold the paper at the top over and squash-fold the middle flap. Then turn the model over.

12.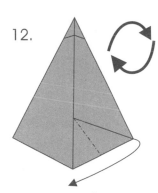

Squash-fold the flap down, then turn the model over.

13.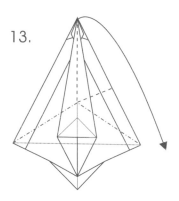

Using an imaginary line between the two points of the side, form a rabbit-ear-fold.

14.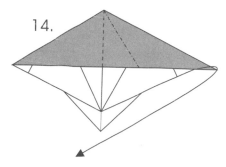

Squash-fold the flap.

15a.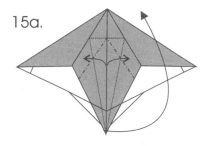

This fold has two stages. Start by opening the pocket in the middle of the flap and swinging the point up.

15b.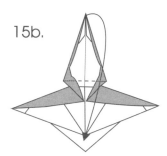

Now fold the flap back down and collapse the flap in on itself as shown.

16.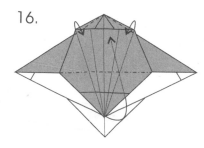

Fold the overlapping paper in, then fold the flap in.

17.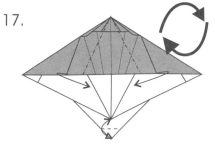

Fold the sides in behind, then turn the model over. Fold the tip as shown then unfold.

18.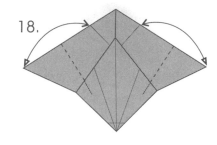

Fold the tips of the flaps to the crease shown and unfold.

19.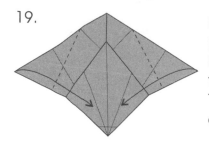

Fold the flaps in perpendicular to their bottom edges using the creases shown. Then turn the model over.

20.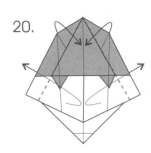

Simultaneously fold the sides in, while swinging the paper behind out.

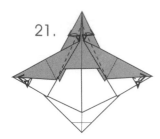

21.

Fold and unfold the creases shown.

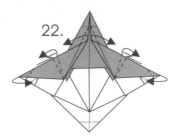

22.

Swivel-fold the wings as shown. Then inside-reverse-fold the wing tips to the crease shown.

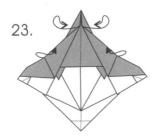

23.

Sink the crimp into the model. You will have to partially unfold the wing for this. Then put the top part of the wings underneath the layers behind them.

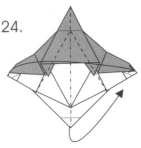

24.

Jet-fold the model by visualizing a line between the top of the wings.

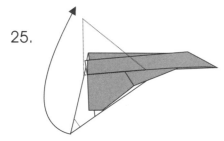

25.

Fold the tail fin up along the bottom edge of the fuselage.

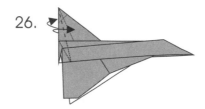

26.

Swivel-fold the rear of the tail fin to the lines in the middle.

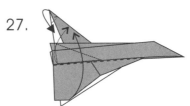

27.

First inside-reverse-fold the tip of the tail fin in, using the preexisting crease. Then fold the excess paper inside as far as it will go. Finally fold the wings up.

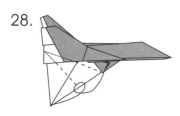

28.

Fold the two flaps over and over to the inside of the model.

29.

Fold the wings out perpendicular to the fuselage.

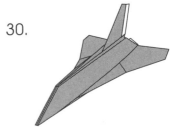

30.

Once this aircraft is properly balanced, it is capable of long flights at high speed. To fly it, grab it at the front of the keel and throw it very hard.

Mako

Use an 8 - 10 inch square of 15 weight paper.

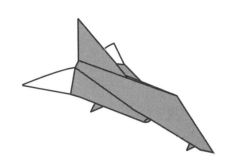

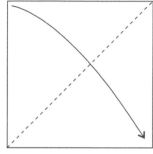

1.

2.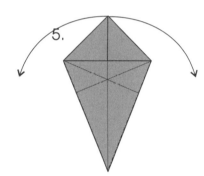

3.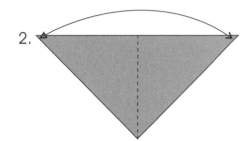

Turn the model over.

4.

Fold the sides down
perpendicular to
edges, then unfold.

5.

Fold the two flaps
down back to step 3.

6.

Using pre-existing creases,
rabbit-ear-fold the paper.

7.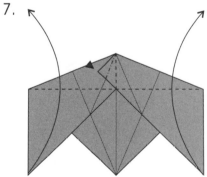

Squash-fold the small flap
down, then fold the two flaps
up. Turn the model over.

8.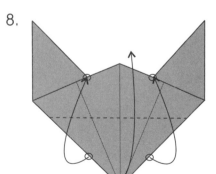

Fold the bottom flap up so
that the edge lines up with
the intersections shown.

9.

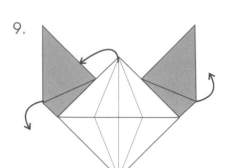

Unfold to step 1.

10.

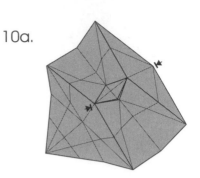

Using preexisting creases, fold the center in on itself and fold the two corners inward.

10a.

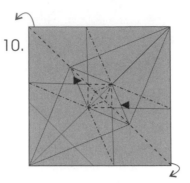

Step 10 in progress.

11.

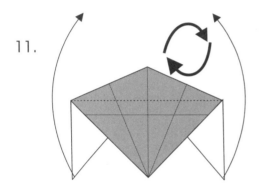

Inside-reverse-fold the two flaps up. Then turn the model over.

12.

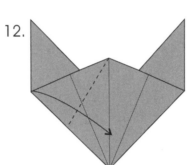

13.

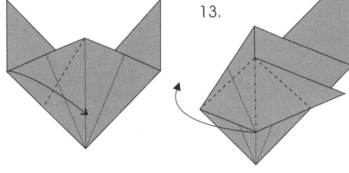

14.

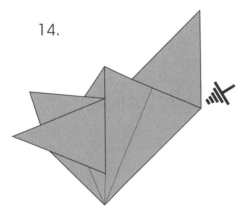

Repeat steps 12 - 14 on the other side.

15.

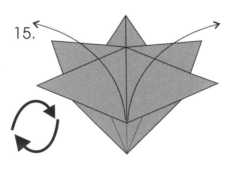

Fold the flaps out, then turn the model over.

16.

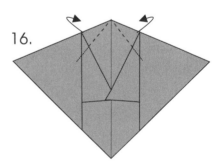

Fold the paper inside as shown. Then return the model to step 15.

17.

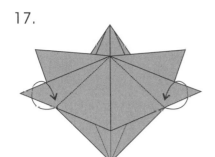

Wrap the paper from behind around.

18.

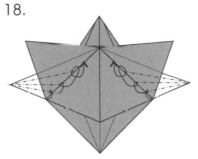

Fold the paper in over and over on top of itself.

19.

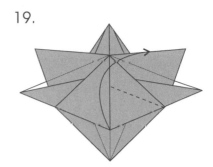

Fold the tip of the flap to the edge as shown.

20.

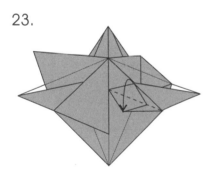

Squash-fold the flap down.

21.

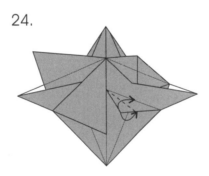

Petal-fold the flap, then fold the point of the top flap to the middle of the petal fold.

22.

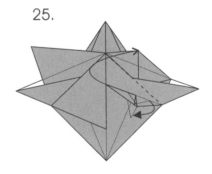

Fold the flap under as shown.

23.

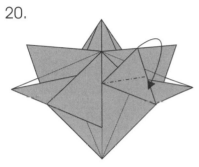

Fold the bottom flap in half.

24.

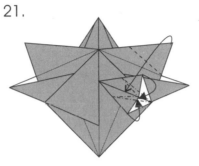

Fold the sides of the flap in to narrow the flap.

25.

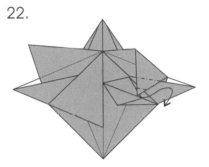

Inside-reverse-fold the small flap out as shown.

26.

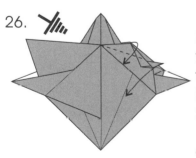

Fold the top of the flap in, then fold the whole flap back to as in step 25. Repeat steps 19 - 26 on the other side.

27.

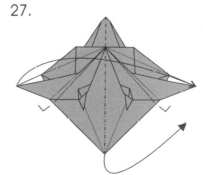

Jet-fold the model.

28.

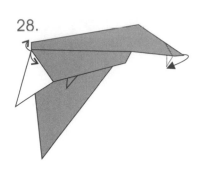

Inside-reverse-fold the small flap in the nose as shown, then open the back of the model so that you can see all of the creases made previously.

29.

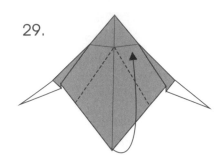

Using the creases made in step 8, inside-reverse-fold the tail fin up.

30.

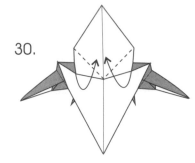

Fold the paper in as shown, then close the model and turn as in step 28.

31.

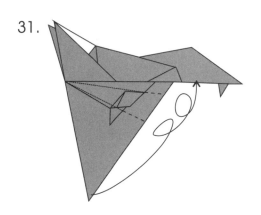

Fold the flap over and over to the inside of the keel to lock the model.

32.

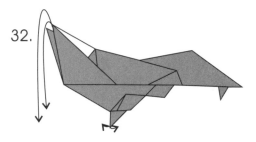

Fold the wings down perpendicular to the fuselage. Then slightly spread the rear landing gear.

33.

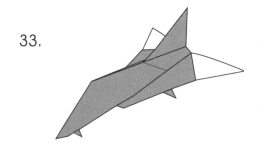

The aircraft should look like this. Grab the plane by the landing gear and give it a firm toss. The landing gear can be retracted and lowered.

Thunderhead

Use an 8 -10 inch square of 15-weight paper .

1.
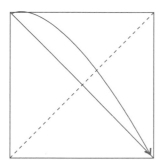

2.
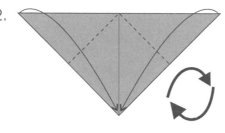

Fold the flaps down and turn the paper over.

3.
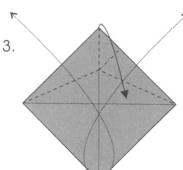

Rabbit-ear-fold the top to the line between the side corners and simultaneously swing the flaps out.

4.
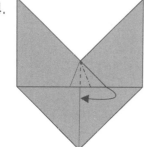

Squash-fold the flap down.

5.
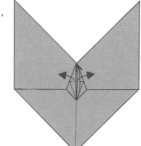

Simultaneously petal-fold the flap and pull the loose paper from the middle out along the fold.

6.
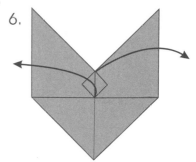

Unfold to step 1.

7.
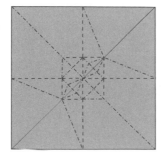

Using the creases you have made, simultaneously fold the paper in on itself as shown. Notice where the mountain- and valley-folds are.

7a.
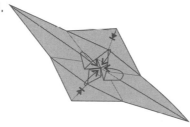

This is step 7 in progress. Notice how the paper is forming and where it is going.

8.
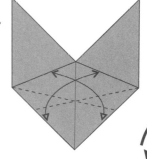

Fold, then unfold as shown, then turn the model over.

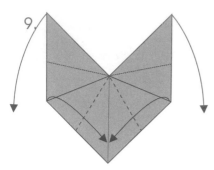

9.

Swivel-fold the points into the center line and fold the top points down. Then turn the model over.

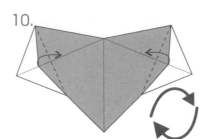

10.

Fold the paper in as shown, then turn the model over.

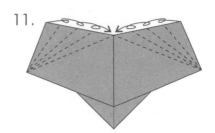

11.

Fold the edges over and over as shown.

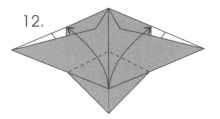

12.

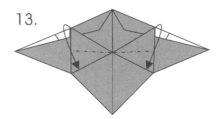

13.

Squash-fold the flaps down.

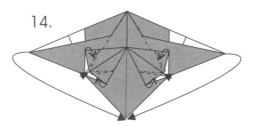

14.

Petal-fold the flaps in. Then inside-reverse-fold the large flaps in.

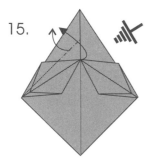

15.

Squash-fold the pocket as shown. A small box pleat will form. Repeat on the other side.

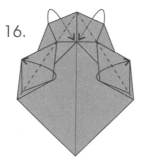

16.

Fold the excess paper into the model. Fold the flaps in half.

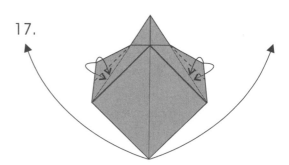

17.

Inside-reverse-fold the two inside flaps out. Then thin the flaps shown with mountain- and valley-folds.

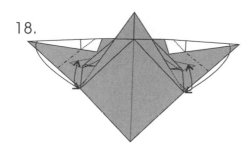

18.

Fold the flaps down through the intersection of the colored and white paper and rotate them so that they meet the bottom corners. Then inside-reverse-fold the small flaps out as shown.

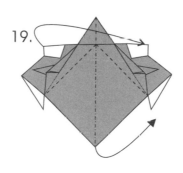

19.

Jet-fold the model.

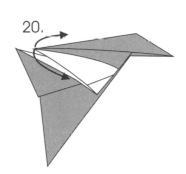

20.

Open out the back of the model so that you can see the creases made in step 8.

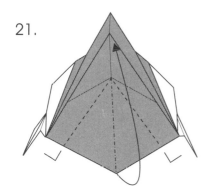

21.

Using the creases made in step 8, inside-reverse-fold the flap so that the rear edge lines up with itself. Then lie the model flat.

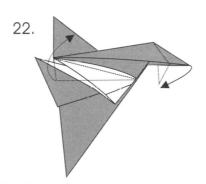

22.

Fold up the excess paper inside the tail fin. Then inside-reverse-fold the small flap down under the nose as shown.

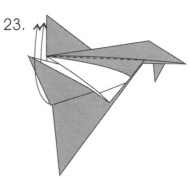

23.

Fold the wings up along the fuselage.

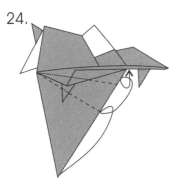

24.

Fold the bottom flap over and over into the model to lock it.

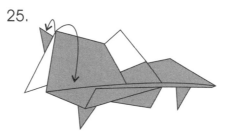

25.

Fold the wings down, perpendicular to the fuselage.

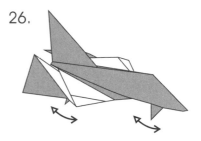

26.

Like the other craft, the landing gear can be lowered and raised. To fly this plane, grab the landing gear and give it a firm toss. It will fly smoothly, and is quite maneuverable.

Stinger

Use an 8-10 inch square 15-weight paper.

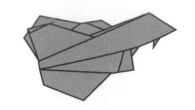

1.

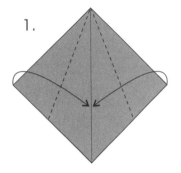

Begin with a preliminary fold. Fold the sides in as shown. Repeat behind.

2.

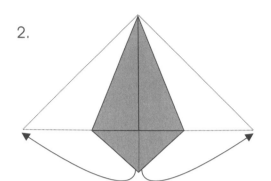

Fold the inner flaps out as for as they will go.

3.

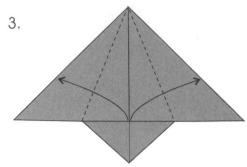

Fold the flaps out. Repeat behind.

4.

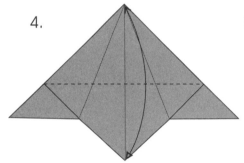

Fold, then unfold.

5.

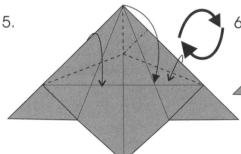

Rabbit-ear-fold the top flap to the line you just made. Then turn the model over.

6.

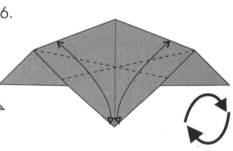

Fold and unfold, then turn the model over.

7.

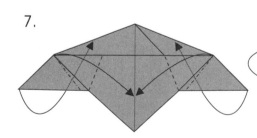

Inside-reverse-fold the large flaps in as shown. Then inside-reverse-fold the small flaps into the center of the model.

8.

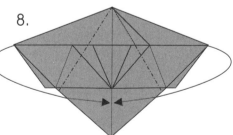

Inside-reverse-fold the sides in.

9.

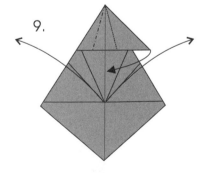

Open out the top of the flap so that it lies on the center line. Then fold the side flaps out as far as they will go.

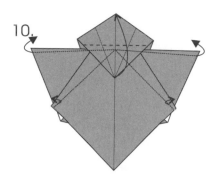

10. Fold the point up to the top of the model. Then shift the excess paper from inside the side flaps out as far as it will go.

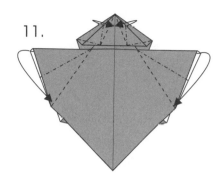

11. Swivel-fold the top flap. Squash-fold the side flaps so that the corner shown lies on the center line.

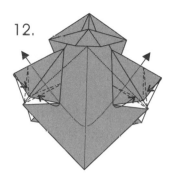

12. Petal-fold the two side flaps. Then inside-reverse-fold the inner flaps using the edges of paper inside and the bottom corners.

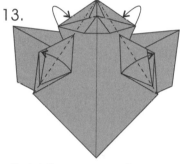

13. Fold the paper shown into the model. Then fold the side flaps in half.

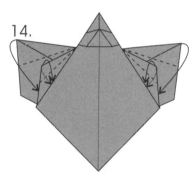

14. Narrow the flaps with valley- and mountain-folds. Then fold the larger flaps as shown.

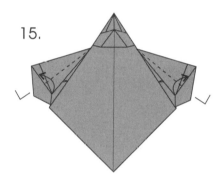

15. Fold the paper over perpendicular to the bottom of the edge as shown.

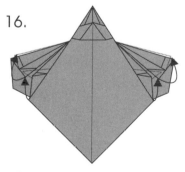

16. Pull the paper out from underneath the fold you just made. Then inside-reverse-fold the small flaps out as shown.

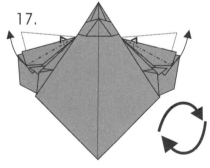

17. Using preexisting creases, pull the top layer of paper and the trapped paper out and stretch it as far as it will go. Then turn the model over.

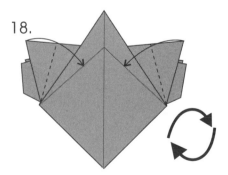

18. Fold the sides into the inner edge. Then turn the model over.

47

19.

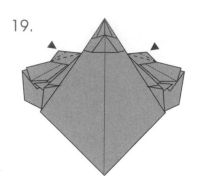

Squash-fold the small areas shown.

20.

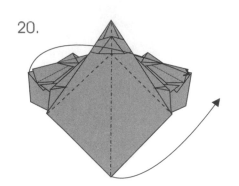

Jet-fold the model using the inner edges.

21.

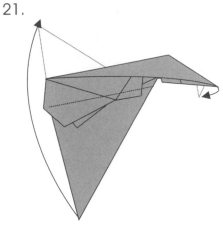

Using the creases made in step 6, inside-reverse-fold the inside flap straight up. Then inside-reverse-fold the small flap under the nose down.

22.

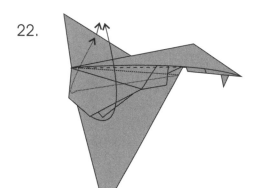

Fold the excess paper from inside the tail fin up. Then fold the wings straight up.

23.

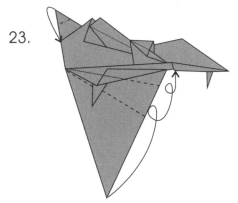

Inside-reverse-fold the tip of the tail fin as shown. Then fold the large bottom flap over and over into the model to lock it.

24.

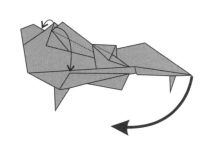

Fold the wings down and turn the model so that the front of the underside of the wings is facing you.

25.

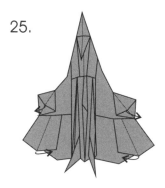

Square off the air intakes and the afterburners by opening them out a little. See step 26.

26.

Rear view.

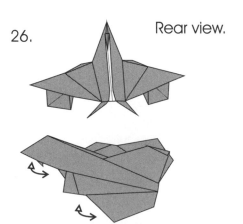

Front view.

Just as with the other craft, the landing gear are fully functional. To fly this plane, grab the rear landing gear and give it a firm throw. This craft is very reliable and is good for dogfighting.

Firebat

Use a 10-inch square of tracing paper.

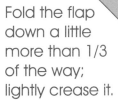

1.

2.

3.

Fold the flap down a little more than 1/3 of the way; lightly crease it.

4.

Lightly fold the bottom point up to the top of the crease you made. If the fold lies completely over the flap you folded down, then crease the first fold. If not repeat steps 3 - 4 until it does.

5.

If the fold resembles this, then unfold to step 3 and inside-reverse-fold the flap in. Repeat behind.

6.

This is what the model should look like. Fold the flap over

7.

8.

Squash-fold the sides to form a modified preliminary fold. Make sure that the white flaps are pointing out of the bottom layers of paper.

9.

Fold only the inside paper in. Then turn the model over.

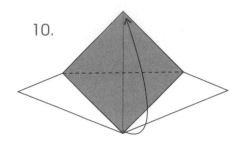

10.

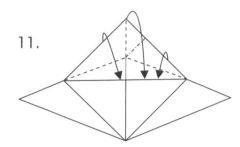

11.

Rabbit-ear-fold the flap.

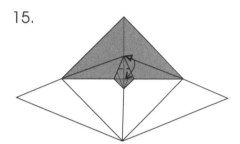

12.

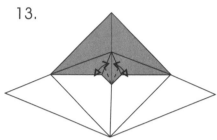

13.

Fold, then unfold the sides of the small flap.

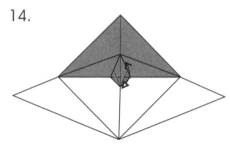

14.

Fold, then unfold the small flap as shown.

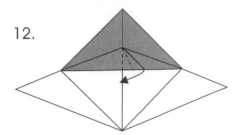

15.

Fold, then unfold the top of the triangle to the line that you just made.

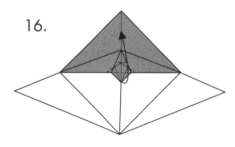

16.

Using the crease you just made, pull the flap up and squash-fold the pockets that form.

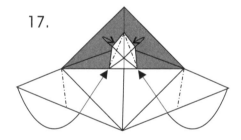

17.

Using the existing creases, fold the sides in on the flap you just made. Then inside-reverse-fold the points of the side flaps to the inner edge as shown.

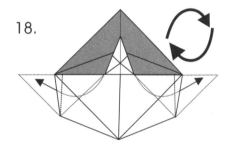

18.

Inside-reverse-fold the flaps as shown. Then turn the model over.

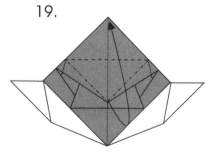

19.

Petal-fold the point up to the top as shown.

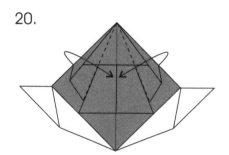

20.

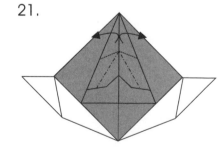

21.

Box-pleat the flaps by opening the small pockets and squash them flat.

50

22.

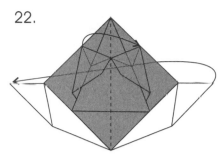

Fold the large flap behind to the opposite flap. Then fold the small flap in the front over.

23.

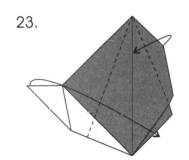

24.

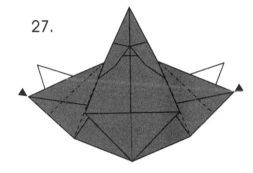

Fold the flap as shown. Repeat behind.

25.

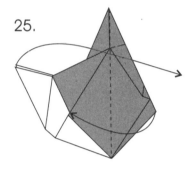

Swing the right top flap to the front and the rear left flap to the back.

26.

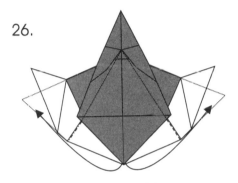

Inside-reverse-fold the inner flaps out along the inside edges of the rear flaps.

27.

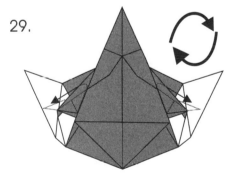

Squash-fold these flaps as shown.

28.

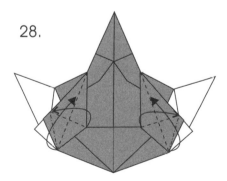

Petal-fold the flap up and then fold it in half.

29.

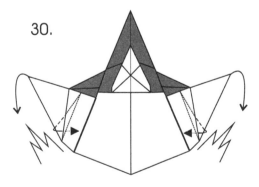

Inside-reverse-fold the flaps out as shown. Then turn the model over.

30.

Swivel-fold the flaps through both layers until they touch the inner edge highlighted.

31.

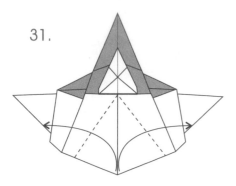

Fold the flaps out from the edge highlighted and swivel them out until they touch the wings as shown.

32.

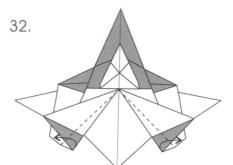

33.

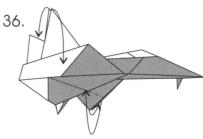

Jet-fold the model as shown.

34.

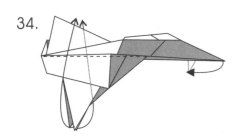

Inside-reverse-fold the small flap under the nose down. Then fold the wings up.

35.

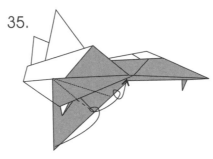

Fold the bottom flap into the model.

36.

Fold the small flaps one over the other into the model. Then fold the wings down perpendicular to the fuselage.

37.

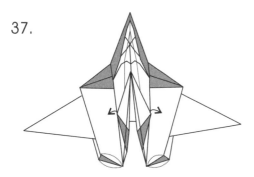

Slightly spread the tail fins. Round the small rear edges of the wings.

38.

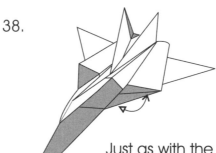

Just as with the other craft, the landing gear can be lowered and raised by inside-reverse-folding them to their original positions and back again. This aircraft will fly with reliability, speed and maneuverability. This plane is arguably the best fighter plane in this book. To fly it, grab the rear landing gear assembly and throw it hard.

Phoenix

Use an 8-10 inch square of 15-weight paper.

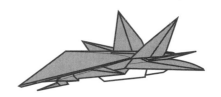

1.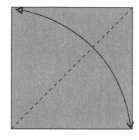

Fold, then unfold.

2.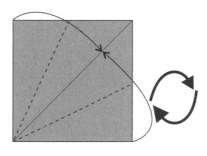

Fold the sides into the center, then turn the model over.

3.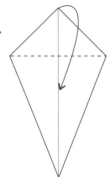

4.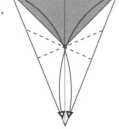

Fold, then unfold, then turn the model over.

5.

6.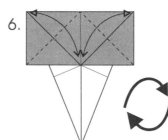

Fold, then unfold, then turn the model over.

7.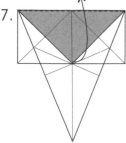

8.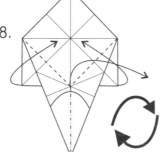

Rabbit-ear-fold the lower flap, then turn the model over.

9.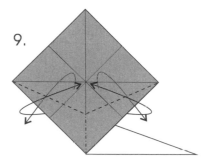

Rabbit-ear-fold the lower half of the square and swing the excess paper from behind out.

53

10.

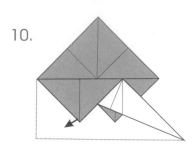

Pull the loose paper down.

11.

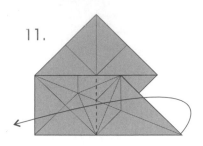

12.

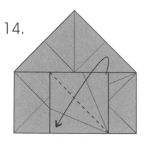

Pull the loose paper down.

13.

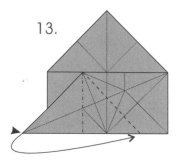

Squash-fold the flap over.

14.

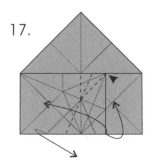

15.

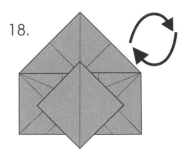

Simultaneously fold the front flap while swinging the rear flap over.

16.

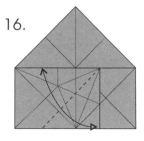

Fold, then unfold.

17.

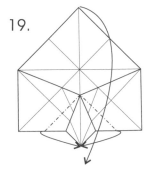

Simultaneously squash-fold the small pocket and swing the flap out to form a diamond. See step 16.

18.

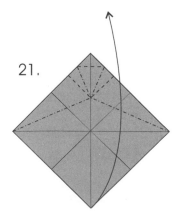

Turn the model over.

19.

Pull the top flap straight down as far as it will go.

20.

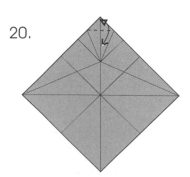

Fold, then unfold.

21.

Petal-fold on the creases made and collapse the large flap.

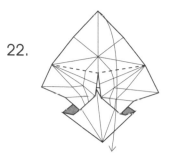

22.

This is step 21 in progress.

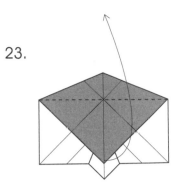

23.

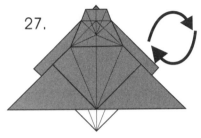

24.

Fold along the existing creases to form a preliminary fold.

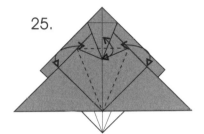

25.

Fold, then unfold.

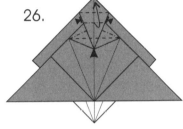

26.

Using preexisting creases and pulling up on the areas indicated, squash-fold the paper shown.

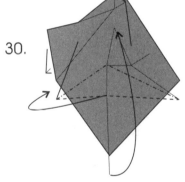

27.

Turn over.

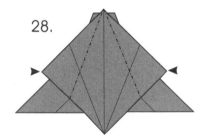

28.

Inside-reverse-fold the two sides in.

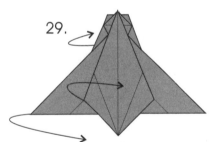

29.

Open out one of the side flaps so that you can see all of the creases on it.

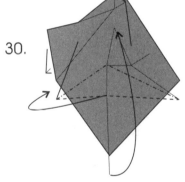

30.

Make the valley-fold, then mountain-fold the paper inward. Keep the model open.

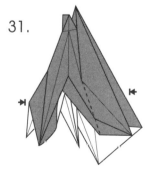

31.

Push the model together and make the indicated fold. Turn the model so the back is facing you.

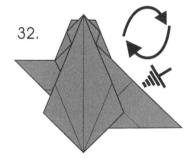

32.

Repeat steps 29 - 31 on the opposite side , then turn the model over.

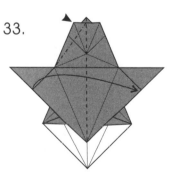

33.

Fold the flap over and squash-fold the paper that won't lie flat.

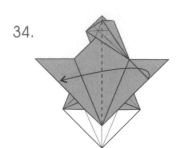

34.

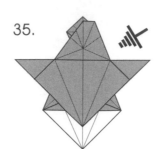

35.

Repeat steps 32 - 34 on the other side.

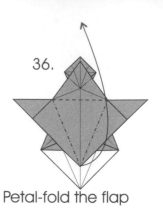

36.

Petal-fold the flap

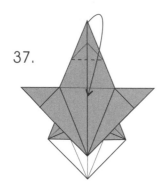

37.

Fold the flap down along the edge behind it.

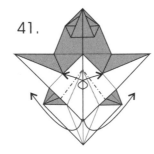

38.

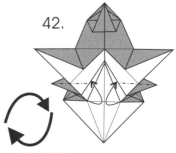

39.

There are four layers on these flaps, inside-reverse-fold between two on each flap.

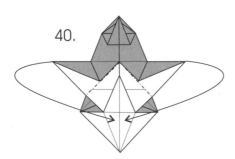

40.

Pull the flaps from underneath out and down.

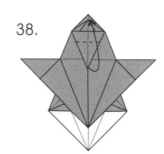

41.

Inside-reverse-fold the flaps out using the edges underneath and the corners on the wings as guides.

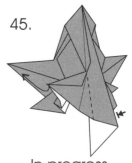

42.

Fold the excess paper in half. Turn the model over.

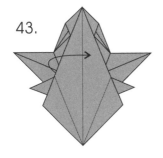

43.

Slightly open out the side of the model.

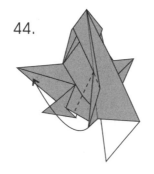

44.

Swivel the bottom flap up using some existing creases.

45.

In progress.

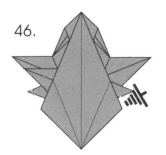

46.

Repeat steps 42 - 45 on the other side.

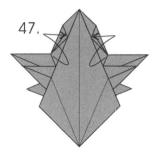

47.

Put these small flaps into the pockets underneath them.

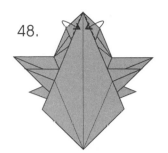

48.

Fold these flaps into the model.

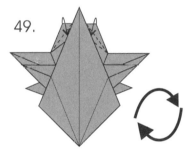

49.

Fold these flaps into the model. Then turn the model over.

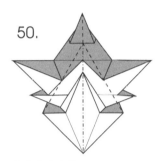

50.

Jet-fold the model as shown.

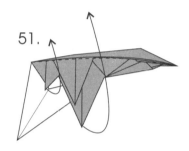

51.

Fold the wings and the tail fins up along the fuselage.

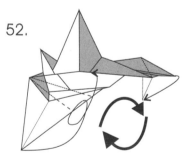

52.

Fold the bottom flap over itself twice. Inside-reverse-fold the flap inside the nose straight down. Turn the model over.

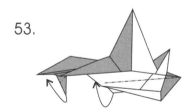

53.

Fold the inner edge made in step 52 inside to the top of the fuselage. Inside-reverse-fold the small flap under the nose to the fuselage.

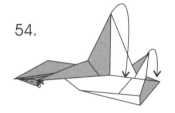

54.

Valley-fold the small flap and open it so that it lies flat against the nose. Fold the wings down perpendicular to the fuselage. Leave the two rudders up a bit. Then turn the model so the back is facing you.

55.

Place one flap inside the other and round them both to form an afterburner. Make sure that the rudders are about 60 degrees from the fuselage.

56.

Turn the model so it faces you.

57.

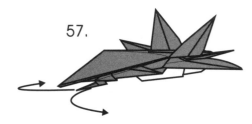

Hold this plane in the front of the keel and give it a smooth moderate toss. It will fly quickly with a good range and with good maneuverability. The small cannon can swivel in a fashion similar to the cannon on the Firestorm.

Cyclone

Use an 8-10 inch square of 15-weight paper.

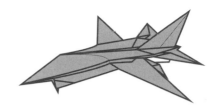

36.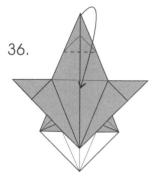

Begin with step 36 of the Phoenix.

37.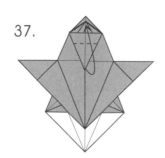

Fold the point to the line that is highlighted.

38.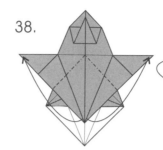

There are four layers on these flaps, inside-reverse-fold between two on each flap.

39.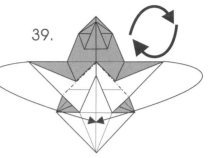

Wrap the flaps from underneath over the flaps above them. Then turn the model over.

40.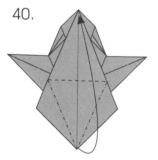

Petal-fold the flap up.

41.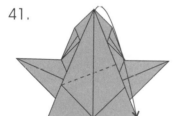

42.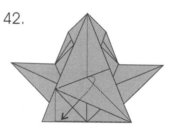

Pull the trapped paper out.

43.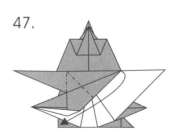

Swivel-fold the flap over.

44.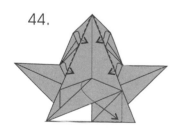

Fold the small flaps of excess paper into the model. Then pull the trapped paper out.

45.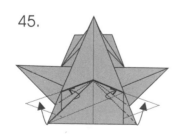

Swivel the inner flaps out so that the lines shown line up with the outer edges. Then turn the model over.

46.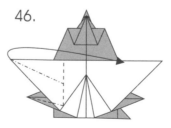

Perform an uneven petal-fold.

47.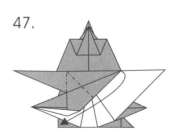

Squash-fold the flap down.

48.

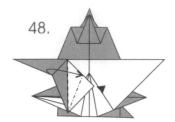

First inside-reverse-fold the flap, then fold it in half.

49.

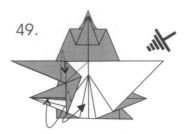
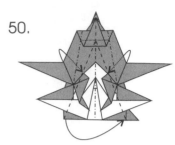

Inside-reverse-fold the small flap as shown. Then fold the excess paper into the model. Finally pull the trapped paper out from inside the flap. Repeat steps 46 - 49 on the other side.

50.

Fold the edges shown into the model. Then perform a modified jet-fold by using an inner edge and the corners shown. Do not crease completely and let the model stay open. Then turn it so the sides are facing you.

51.

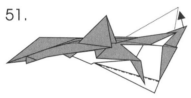

Pull the inner flap up so that what will be the bottom reaches the edges shown.

52.

Roll the two innermost flaps together into the model. Then inside-reverse-fold the small flap down as shown. Round the areas shown by pushing in. Rotate the plane so that the rear is facing you.

53.

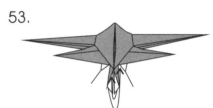

Place one flap inside the other and then place the other flap over the top. Form an afterburner by rounding and opening the space between.

54.

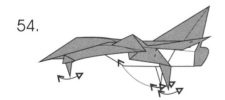

To raise the rear landing gear swivel them up as shown. You can lower them by swiveling them back. The front landing gear can be raised and lowered with inside-reverse-folds.

55.

To fly this plane, grab the front of the keel and give it a smooth, firm toss. This plane is capable of long flights and is quite maneuverable.

Flight Instructions

General Instructions:

Due to the compact design of these aircraft, they do not fly like any other aircraft and as such must be flown differently. As a general rule, to hold these aircraft properly grab the keel with your thumb, index finger, and middle finger. Note the illustration below.

Throw the planes in a smooth and consistent manner. The nose of the aircraft must be pointing in the direction that it is being thrown, otherwise it will not function properly. Note the picture below.

When you release the aircraft, you must release both sides of the keel at the same time. If you do not, the plane will veer to the side that was released last. For practice, simply throw the aircraft up in the air with a little force, so that you understand how the aircraft flies. I recommend you try this before moving on.

Maneuvers:

Banking

In order to bank, or turn, the aircraft you must throw the aircraft with a tilt either left or right, and with some force. Note the pictures below.

Left bank.   Right bank.

The plane will then turn in the direction that you tilt it. The greater you tilt it the sharper the turn will be.

Skimming

A skim is similar to a bank except it is more difficult to accomplish. When performed successfully, the aircraft will dart at the ground and pull up before hitting. To do this you must throw the aircraft at the ground with a good amount of force. Note the picture below.

Balancing:

In order for the aircraft to fly properly, you must balance it. To balance the aircraft you must ensure that both sides of the aircraft are pulling with the same force. You may have to lower or raise an edge of the wing to balance it out, or move an edge of a tail fin left or right. This can be determined by watching which way the plane flies.

Troubleshooting:

The craft will fly properly when all of the edges are symmetrical, however this is more the exception than the rule, so you may need to troubleshoot.

If the plane is pulling up to the right, then either lower the right trailing edge or raise the left trailing edge. Note the picture below.

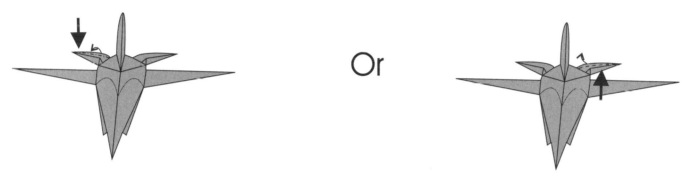

Or

If the plane is pulling up to the left, then either lower the left trailing edge or raise the right trailing edge. Note the picture below.

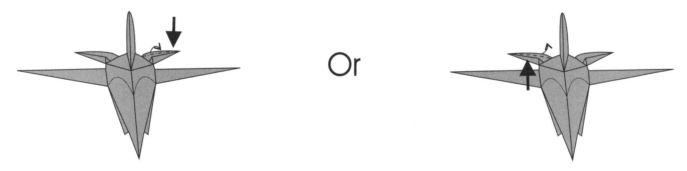

Or

If the aircraft is turning to the left then bend the tail fin(s) to the right. Note the picture below.

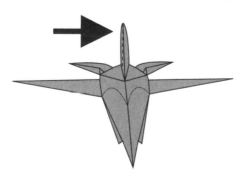

If the aircraft is turning to the right, then bend the tail fin(s) to the left. Note the picture below.

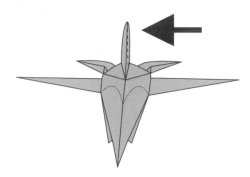

Some of these aircraft seem like they will never fly, but with enough time and patience, you can correct any problem. Good luck and enjoy.